The *Egg* Principle of Leadership

Charles A. Ford

Kingdom Builders Publications LLC

© 2017 Charles A. Ford
Kingdom Builders Publications, LLC

All rights reserved. No part of this book may be reproduced or transmitted in any form or by any means without written permission from the author.

Printed in the USA

ISBN: 9780692935361

Library of Congress Control Number: 2017912565

Authored by
Charles Allen Ford

Editor
KBPLLC Editorial Staff
Donald Lee

Photographer

Cover Design
LoMar Designs

Scripture quotations marked KJV are taken for the HOLY BIBLE KING JAMES VERSION
www.biblegateway.com

This Book Belongs to

DEDICATION

To my wife, *Apostle Juanita Ford*, who's authored two books herself and has played a vital role in my life. She sees inside me an ability to write books and help develop others be the best they can be. I thank my wife of 40 years. Her books are **Life in the Blood** and **Victory Through the Blood.**

Juanita, YOU WILL ALWAYS BE IN MY "VISION!"

"Where there is no vision, the people perish."
Proverbs 29:18 (KJV)

The *Egg* Principle of Leadership

CONTENTS

	Dedication	iv
	Acknowledgment	vii
	Introduction	10
1	The Ostrich Egg and Leadership	13
2	The Alligator and the Leader	17
3	The Snapper Turtle and the Leader	20
4	The Eagle and the Leader	23
5	The Emu and the Leader	28
6	The Chicken and the Leader	31
	Epilogue	34
	About the Author	36

Charles A. Ford

The *Egg* Principle of Leadership

ACKNOWLEDGMENTS

This book is dedicated to my father and mother, both of whom are deceased; Curtis Lincoln Ford and Doris Mildred Ford (Hynson). I am grateful to be in the land of the living. If it had not been for you both, there would not be a CHARLES ALLEN FORD.

To my brothers and sisters; Curtis Harold Ford, Mary Ann Littlejohn, Diann Oliver King, Peggy Lee White, and Harold Leroy Ford, thank you for the support you have given me over the years.

Ministers who made a difference in my life; Brother and Sister Barnard, Missionaries and mentors, Pastors Lucius and Teresa Toney, Pastors Creflo A. and Taffi Dollar, Pastors

Connis R. and Ruby Jackson, Apostles Henry and Ann Jones, Apostles Gregory and Junie Kelley, Pastor Lee and family, Sharon Hope Handed, Yolanda Allison; Sister by adoption, and all of my spiritual sons and daughters, and my supporters.

Military Comrades; thanks to the many different leaders who, throughout my 21-year military career, made a great impact in my life.

Last, but not least, thank you to Kingdom Builders Publications, under the leadership of my mother of publishing; the publisher, Louise Smith. We're thankful to her for the service she renders and the patience she showed my spouse and me.

Question: What is the difference between Charles' first journey and his second?
Answer:
LEADERSHIP

INTRODUCTION

Understanding the purpose of
a thing helps us to explore
what has not been uncovered.
~*Charles A. Ford*

Now we want to introduce to you the parallel of the animal kingdom and how it relates to human leadership in our everyday life. It has come to my attention through many years of study and even applying these basic principles in my everyday life.

I will show you how each animal does the following:

- Goes through basically the same process of development
- Each animal produces eggs to give

birth to the next generation
- How each animal leaves its own personality on that which it sits on.

Observe the process, reproduction, and personality of each egg being developed. Watch the closeness of its relationship to the human development process.

Before we start this quest on looking for leadership development, I will begin with a question.

Questions to Ask Yourself

- What Do I Allow to Sit on Me?
- If I were to present someone with an egg and then ask what he has in his hand, his response would probably be the same as most others, an egg. But, on the contrary, it could not be just an egg because there is something still inside the shell that needs to come out.

That something requires its kind to sit on it in order for full development. Is that right? Answer this question for yourself.

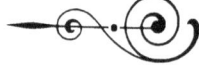

THE OSTRICH EGG AND THE LEADER
Chapter One

Understanding the process of certain things sometimes gives us more insight why the effect of one thing is greater than that of another.

- The ostrich (the hen) lays between 12 to 15 eggs, laying one egg every other day. The nest for her eggs is a shallow hole in the ground. Both the female and male ostrich sit on the eggs as they incubate.
- In comparison to the chicken egg, the hard shell of an ostrich egg cannot just be cracked or peeled. The shell, which resembles ceramic, is approximately 1/8 of an inch thick. The female ostrich sits on the egg during the day and the male takes over at night. Therefore, the egg has to be

strong enough to support up to 400 pounds. One ostrich egg can serve up to 15 people. But before you can cook with the egg, you have to be able to crack it.

NOTE: Ostriches lay on average between 40 and 100 eggs per year, and each egg takes 42 days to hatch. In the wild, or on farms where the ostriches can hatch their own eggs, the females will sit on the nests during the days and at night the males take over. If you are looking to raise ostrich eggs yourself, however, you will need to follow a few steps to ensure that your eggs successfully hatch.

Ostrich eggs are big. Each egg weighs as much as 2.5 pounds and is approximately 6 inches long. The shell of the egg is 0.06 of an inch in thickness. Yet it is capable of supporting the weight of a person, according to Wonderquest.com. The biggest ostrich egg on record weighed 5 pounds, 2 ounces and was laid in 1988 in Israel.

Let's look at the "leadership" of a human being. Notice that the ostrich only has the ability to reproduce who he or she is on the inside. I would like to make this statement:

"Only what is in a leader can be produced in any environment." It is not fair to ask the leader to produce what has not been developed within him or her.

Exodus 18:13-25 (King James Version) Moses, with the advice of his father-in-law, gave some instructions based on the ability of the men in his camp. The directives were for the purpose of helping to make Moses' assignment easier.

Perhaps you can tell from reading my life's story that it takes the right style of leadership to "sit on you so that you can be all you can be."

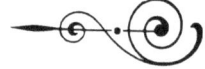

THE ALLIGATOR AND THE LEADER
Chapter Two

It takes the embryos from sixty-three to eighty-four days to be ready to hatch, depending on the temperature inside the nest. The embryos, like the adults, need heat from their surroundings for energy to grow and develop. But no matter how long it takes her offspring to develop, the female stays on guard. The mother alligator will also lunge to scare away enemies, such as raccoons or bears. Those animals would like to dig up alligator eggs for dinner.

NOTE: Life is dangerous for a baby alligator. It spends much of its time hunting for food in shallow water. Only one of every ten alligators lives through its first year. Those are not good odds. By the time it is two years old, the young alligator will be big enough to have fewer enemies.

The alligator will grow rapidly for the first five or six years and then continue growing slowly for the rest of its life. Alligators are fascinating. They are among the most powerful reptiles. We do not need to fear alligators, but we must respect them.

Again, leaders can begin their process of development just like the alligator, and be under someone that has the same spirit of the alligator. This type of leadership will not back down from anything and will not allow the babies to grow. However, if these leaders have received the Holy Spirit and walk in the fruit of the Spirit, they can produce great leaders who are strong, yet humble. (See *Acts 6:1-7*.)

Look back over your life and see how many people have influenced you over the years and have made great deposits in terms of helping you to be the best you that you can be. I am sure you can see in yourself a glimpse of someone you admired and looked up to.

THE SNAPPING TURTLE AND THE LEADER
Chapter Three

Snapping turtles have fierce dispositions. However, when encountered in the water they usually slip quietly away from any disturbance. This breed of turtles will snap in self-defense because, unlike other turtles, they are too large to hide in their own shells when confronted. These turtles rarely bite humans; they usually flee when threatened.

NOTE: The snapper is an aquatic ambush hunter, capturing its prey with its beak-like jaws.

Eggs and Hatchlings

Female snapping turtles lay 20 to 40 eggs in open sand or vegetation, and the eggs incubate for around 100 days. After incubation, the hatchlings emerge and hide in nearby water. Hatchling common snapping turtles are only an inch in length when they emerge, and hatchlings are extremely susceptible to predation.

Zero to Four Years

After hatchlings emerge and begin feeding on insects, small fish, crustaceans, and other small animals, they gain diameter and weight. In the first four years of growth, snapping turtles will grow from one to six inches in diameter. Weight is more variable based on the time of year and the diet of the individual turtle. But on average, young turtles weigh 10 to 15 pounds and have an average carapace diameter of one to 10 inches.

NOTE: Because of the long lifespan of the snapping turtle, growth is very slow and intermittent. Turtles enter hibernation in late autumn and do not emerge until spring. So growth stops during the winter months.

Charles A. Ford

"THE PROCESS, GROWTH, AND DEVELOPMENT OF EACH ANIMAL ARE DIFFERENT AND CARRY WITH IT THE ABILITY ONLY TO PRODUCE AFTER ITS OWN KIND."

Example of the human nature in comparison with the animal kingdom

There are some people who grew up in their family house. Because of something discomforting that may have happened in that environment in their past, they snap at other people

Example:
It was hard for me, coming from a family that drank and partied every weekend and where fights would break out, accompanied by cursing and knives and bottles being thrown. As a child, it messed with my temperament from time to time. But it also impacted how I would relate to other people. I learned how to remain calm under pressure, also because of having to live in that kind of surrounding.

Children learn a lot from the environment they grow up in, watching and taking notes in their hearts and minds.

The *Egg* Principle of Leadership

THE EAGLE AND THE LEADER
Chapter Four

Let's examine "The Eagle and the Leader Principle" and see how it relates to the natural leader in human beings.

I. The Eagles
The eagles will often build their nest in the tallest tree available. This helps them to watch for danger. A young eagle gains up to 4 ounces (113g) of insight in a single day.

II. The Care of the Eaglets
(Three things to observe about the Eagle)
a. Brooding (Genesis 1:1, John 16:13)

Young eaglets are born with a coat of soft, fluffy called DOWN, and they cannot keep themselves warm. One of the parents (ministry gifts according to

Ephesians 4:7-16), must CROUCH, down in the nest, keeping the young (believers) warm from rain, wind, or cold weather (being ejective from adverse conditions). This behavior is known as (BROODING).

    b. Defensive Mechanism

Eagles as parents (Spiritual Parents) must be on guard against predators or other eagles that will prey on helpless eaglets (new believers or Christians). The young grow strong because of the attentiveness or the development process of the leader.

NOTE: The parents (leaders) of the eaglets (believers) sit by the nest (schools, homes, church, business, or jobs) looking at all enemies that approach the eaglets or new believer nest. Read Psalm 91:1-16

Parents rip up the prey (food) into small pieces so the eaglets or (believers) can devour the food substance for them to digest it.

Feedings take place every 3 to 4

hours for eaglets. After 6 to 7 weeks, the parents' (overseers, leaders) job gets easier because the eaglets can rip up the prey themselves.

c. Imprinting and Bonding Process
Newly hatched eaglets go through a process known as "IMPRINTING."

Within a few days of hatching, young bald eagles imprint on the sight and sound of their parents. They do not recognize their parents specifically. Instead, they learn to identify the adults as their own kind. Once an eaglet has imprinted on its parents, it will accept food from any other bald eagle.

Imprinting is an important part of an eagle's life. By recognizing and watching others of its kind, an eagle learns how to behave like a survivor in its environment.

Note: When young bald eagles are ready to mate, they will look for partners that resemble their parents.

III. Development Process

a. Eaglets – A newly hatched eaglet does not look anything like its parents. After about 4 hours, it will open its eyes for the first time. By three weeks of age, the young bird weighs about 5 pounds and is a foot high. Eaglets or new born-again Christians normally squabble with one another over food (Scriptures).

b. Fledglings – Bald eagles fledge, or learn to fly 8 to 14 weeks after hatching.

Investigating these animals in their environment gives us a different look at the animal kingdom in comparison with humans to some degree. It will be necessary to note what kind of leaders we are producing in our different types of environments that we live in.

We have discovered that to be the best you must understand what you have before you. I have learned as a leader that if you know the principle of something you will always make the best product.

From April of 1978 to the present, I have been blessed to train for the military and share with many churches the principles of leadership. I plan to release more into the kingdom of God for the benefit of His kingdom.

Notice that the eagles have great achievements because of their growth process. They have one ability I love to observe, and that is their flight above storms or even into them when necessary. They also train their young to soar, fly higher, and take a beating. And lastly, they know when it is time to pluck the old feathers and get renewed in their own strength. Wouldn't you like to have a leader like that in your life, one who will keep pushing you to greater heights?

THE EMU AND THE LEADER
Chapter Five

The emu is the second-largest largest bird in the world by height, after its ratite relative, the ostrich. It is endemic to Australia where it is the largest native bird and the only extent member of the genus emus.

Emus are soft-feathered, brown, flightless birds with long necks and legs, and can reach up to 6.2 feet in height. Emus can travel great distances and, when necessary, can sprint 30 mph. They forage. They drink infrequently, but take in large amounts of water when the opportunity arises.

Breeding takes place in May and June, and fighting among females for a mate is common. Females can mate several times and lay several clutches of eggs in one season. The male does the incubation. During this process, he hardly eats or drinks and he loses a significant amount of weight. The eggs hatch after around eight weeks, and the young are nurtured by their fathers. They reach full size after around six months, but can remain as a family unit until the next breeding season. The emu is an important cultural icon of Australia, appearing on various coins. The bird features prominently in Indigenous Australian mythology.

Let's compare the leadership qualities of both emus and human beings.

*First, you can see that anything being released from the male and female emu will have an advantage over many because of their speed and height.

A man and his wife are like an emu and his mate in that humans, like the emus, will bring forth many who will have great vision. Anyone who learns from observing these animals can have a great leadership team. They will have the ability to look from great heights and the vision can be seen from afar.

When you evaluate the characteristics of these animals, you're likely to see that they can offer insight into many things. Each animal has a style of leadership that, when emulated, can make a mark in our society.

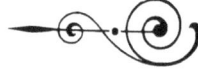

THE CHICKEN AND THE LEADER
Chapter Six

I'd like to ask this question again. If you had an egg in your hand, what do you have? Do you have just an egg or do you have an underdeveloped egg?

Here, we have a chicken. All chickens come from hens. So, it is essential to understand that all eggs need a hen sitting on it. Equally so, as it relates to humans, everyone needs someone to "sit on him," or motivate him to reach his maximum potential.

Keep in mind that the only reason we have eggs in the store or super market is because somebody removed them before their full potential could develop. If we are to become what we want to be, we must sit under the right people.

More information on hens and eggs:

- Female chicks are called pullets for their first year or until they begin to lay eggs. For most breeds, around 20 weeks is a typical age for their first egg.
- Some breeds lay eggs daily, some, every other day, and some once or twice a week.
- Some hens never lay eggs because of their narrow pelvises or other anomalies.
- Normal laying routines can be interrupted by molting, winter daylight shortage, extreme temperatures, illness, poor nutrition, stress or lack of fresh water. Hens usually return to normal labor habits when the disruption-causing factor is corrected.

Again, we can learn a lot from the nature of birds. Metaphorically drawing from birds, look at what you want to become. Then pursue your dream. There is somebody positioned to help you become that.

You can only become what you submit yourself to. In other words, if you aspire to be great, be willing to learn from someone who is already that. In doing so, you will become a great leader.

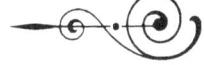

EPILOUGE

As I conclude my thoughts, the over goal in this book is to think about our future; with our families, school systems, community, states, churches, and the world at large.

The purpose of this book is to allow leaders to think about the legacy that will impact the generation before us. We will make our mark through opportunities that will not be erased in their lives.

Leaders must keep in mind the structure and culture of the animals talked about in the previous chapters. Animals still make their life count, however, they can still be changed and tamed (cause and affect).

Make a challenge to sharpen yourself and help the advancement of the upcoming generation. Examine your style of follow-ship and/or leadership. Remember, we are constantly growing and changing. Get prepared, be ready, and stay in fortitude for where you will go and know your leadership will influence nations, but the choice is yours on how you will impact them. I hope you will choice positive and righteous stimuluses.

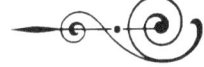

ABOUT THE AUTHOR

Charles Allen Ford is the remaining child of a  twin birth. They were born in Chestertown, Maryland. His twin succeeded him in death at birth. Charles was reared and educated in Wilmington, Delaware. While in high school, he wrestled under the leadership of Coach Seabrook. Charles under his wing, Charles at 98 pounds competed at state for three years. His military career afforded Ford to have his own wrestling team.

Charles retired from the United States Army after 21 years. Reflecting over his life, Charles notes that he appreciates the time he spent with great leaders who helped him to grow and become the man he is today.

In S.H.A.P.E. (Supreme Headquarters Allied Power Europe), Belgium in March 1976 (United States Army).

March, 1980 (Killeen, Texas) began his ministerial training.

From that, he accepted his call as an

Apostle, June 1999. He has traveled the world preaching the gospel in Texas, South Carolina, Alabama (where we started a Cell Group), Georgia, North Carolina, Delaware, Pennsylvania, Florida, Korea, Germany, to list a few.

He re-entered the military with the Army National Guard in 1974. He finished basic training and Advanced Individual Training (AIT) at Fort Jackson, South Carolina as a clerk typist.

The only way he could stay in the Army the second time around, ironically, as Charles explains, was to take it when his drill sergeant "*sat on me.*" To this day, Charles says, he's grateful for his D.S. leadership ability.

Ford encountered a young lady name Juanita Lovett, who would one day become his wife. She also was in the communication field. Charles didn't know Juanita was a switchboard operator. He was also a switchboard operator. She invited him to church, led him to the altar, where he encountered his first experience with the Lord, then they started their journey.

Their connection would have such a profound affect and has spanned some 40 years.

Her tenacity became a part of his success story. Feb. 14, 1977, Charles asked Juanita for her hand in marriage. She said, "YES," and on June 18, 1977, they were married.

Charles A. Ford

Charles says if he had not married Juanita Lovett, his life would not have gone in the direction it has. It all boils down to her "leadership" ability and his willingness to allow her to be a developer in his life.

www.ingramcontent.com/pod-product-compliance
Lightning Source LLC
Chambersburg PA
CBHW042054290426
44110CB00006B/179